# FELDSPAR

By the same author:

*Why I am Not a farmer*
*A Paddock in His Head*
*A Tight Circle*
*Travelling Through the Family*
*Small Town Soundtrack*
*The Lowlands of Moyne*
*Walk like a Cow (Memoir)*

# FELDSPAR

## BRENDAN RYAN

RECENT
WORK
PRESS

Feldspar
Recent Work Press
Canberra, Australia

Copyright © Brendan Ryan, 2023

ISBN: 9780645651270 (paperback)

 A catalogue record for this
book is available from the
National Library of Australia

Cover image: 'Mawsitsit (chromian jade)' by James St John, 2014. Reproduced under
Creative Commons 2.0 licence
Cover design: Recent Work Press
Set by Recent Work Press

recentworkpress.com

PH

*For my parents*

# Contents

## Arrival points

Feldspar 3
The Parents 5
Sonnets for a mother 7
Watching the news 10
What I return to and miss 12
A tin kettling 15
The potato bag needle 16
Mostly 18
Hanging out the washing 19
Self-seeded 20

## Signatures

Wimmera light 23
The Stick Shed of Murtoa 24
Wimmera junk 25
Driving through mallee towns 26
Bleached paddocks 27
Language of rubs 28
A taste for blood 29
Between the pen and the roundabout 31
A squeeze of paddocks 32
Mushrooms 33
Between a paddock and a hayshed 34
The flattened grass patches 35
Undertow 36
Signatures 38
Drive 39

## Taking it slow

Park life 43
Petrichor 46
Waiting for my daughter to finish work 47
She plugs in 48
I do this, I do that 49
The ineffable 50

The explosion                              51
Skinheads                                  52
What we did to each other                  53
Taking it Slow                             56
Hurt                                       58
Dirt                                       59
Arumpo Road                                60

## Lament

All her glories                            65
Tell it                                    67
You                                        68
True                                       69
Anniversary Poem                           71
At the lake's edge                         72
Contentions                                73
Turning my back on Australians overseas    74
Soon there will be townhouses              75
The truck driver's lament                  76
The invigilator's dream                    78
And                                        80
Midnight Oil at Mt Duneed                  82
Here                                       84

# Arrival points

# Feldspar

In a dark light, edges of the granite
begin to shine. A breeze is rocking boats
but the blue gums are barely moving.

Through the lounge window, the mountain
looks back at me framed by how I've been
sizing up mountains since I was a child—

of being chased by shadows
inching across paddocks like spilt ink.
The light shifts and the pink hue of feldspar

catches my eye, reminding me
it is not parents who change but the way
we see them age, sometimes uncomfortably.

Sometimes there is only time to think
when my body is in motion, falling into a rhythm
of words, stubbing my toe on tree roots

the swaying farmer's walk. I trudge on behind you
and the lives of people we rarely see
those deaths we learn about on holidays

other camping trips merge with seed pods
on gravelly paths. We step around hollow logs
pull branches away from our eyes

carry the voices of people sometimes reluctantly
like rubbing a wattle leaf between fingers
then dropping it absent-mindedly

words falling and rising with a dirt path
hooked and twisted branches scattered about us.
I follow your breaths around rocks, uphill

to a view where there is no news, no media
and we are not the centre of the world.
The family I have left behind

and what that means here, beyond arrival points.
Feldspar, banksia, swamp melaleauca
drawing me in like breaths to count the day to.

# The Parents

Any night finds them earthed
before a stack of Irish CDs resting
near the bottom of the screen.

An eco-system of newspapers, pens,
walking stick, half-opened Quick-Eze
scattered about them. What falls to me

when I look at my father's face—
memory lines scored by skin cancers
his perpetual ageing grin.

He steps bow-legged towards the fridge.
A litre and a half of soda water
blister pack of coloured pills

and he is pushing his chair back
from the table, fox-eyed.
My mother reads local newspapers into the night.

Footy scores ignite her. She takes out
her hearing aid to doze, talk on the phone
*Go on with you, you're a good one to talk.*

My father offers a conspiratorial smile
later, confides, *she's the best little worker
I've known.*

Subdued muttering from a radio in a bedroom.
Roast chicken, pasta salad, beetroot slices in a bowl.
These images of my parents I carry on repeat.

A lifetime of farming has come down to this—
sitting in an upright chair watching the races
pushing a walker one hundred metres to a milk bar.

All his life my father has stared at boundary fences
now he watches the footpath for a familiar face.
Each day, their victory is to wake, swing out of bed

my parents carry paddocks between their chairs
cow lines trail their glances. They have never flown
overseas or boarded a cruise ship.

Berthed in two lounge chairs, they watch the footy
bouncing off each other like commentators.
They can't believe how lucky they are.

# Sonnets for a mother

i

She was always staying up late, pottering
around, folding clothes, reading a newspaper
before an open fire. The grandfather clock
swung to a rhythm my mother padded to at night
rising from a chair to put the kettle on.
She always opened up with a cup of tea and biscuits
her hands clasped behind her head
admitting to wisdoms I couldn't prepare for.

Even now with her radio or TV footy shows turned up
I know what it is to sit beside her
listening to the talk that goes on; who's coming down
to visit, who won't be there at Christmas.
All our lives, we've given her so much to stay up late for.
The sound of her voice worth sitting down to.

ii

She taps hers fingers on the table when she talks
each corrected thought beats like a syllable count.
She pauses, backtracks, draws out her vowels
for emphasis bouncing between forefinger
and thumb—who Auntie Gladys married
the rhythms of her past dancing amongst bread crumbs.

Of suitors, she had a few before getting word to my father
she couldn't meet him on the steps of St Josephs.
Her own father, dead that morning—it wasn't a story,
although once at The Dances she snapped at a question
*no thanks, I'd rather go out with my girlfriends.*
Loyal to St Kilda, she left her job the day she married—
*It was just something you did.* Lost to the back and forth of tennis
our talk fast becoming background music.

iii

At a young age I learnt that it was better to lie
than to walk down the street imagining I was somebody else.
Once I feigned the flu for a week until you discovered
the bully that kept me sweating beneath the sheets.
I felt like something cornered by a truth I was trying to postpone.
I walked around with my eyes closed so that I might be forgotten.
You listened in between washing and cooking, bearing witness
with a tea towel, dishing up steaks, talking the way families do.

Your voice on the phone brought the paddocks
back home to me. The way you recounted each football match
each brother and sister—checkpoints in a list repetitive as prayer.
One night I listened and cried from a Mildura telephone box.
The next week I drove six hours to watch you folding clothes.
I am who I am, one day I will graduate from you, alone.

# Watching the news

My mother's hands are quivering.
When she speaks she rubs her thighs, hips
sometimes she forgets, other times she remembers
by dancing her fingers on a table in front of her.
There is a distance between us we bridge
with phone calls. It is like watching the news
imagining I am informed.

Arthritis swells and stiffens my thumbs.
I've lost strength, can't twist some bottles.
Each hand folds in. To stretch
is to push back the webbing, expose
the lines that persist.
My father's hands are calcified, swollen
from years of milking cows or punching wool
from dead sheep. They hang from him like machines
out of use, blotched as old maps. He blows on the corners
when he turns the pages of a newspaper.

Each conversation becomes a portrait of my own ageing.
There is back story to their silences, expected answers
the way my mother stands close to him outside Mass.
They don't want pity, attention or to talk about doctors
but they do.
My father discusses his pacemaker battery with his brother.
It is a bedrock conversation that measures their honesty
by the way they clasp their hands at the table.

Each time I am with them, I become a different person.
I find my way by their politics, side-stepping the bait
I return to shouting with their friends about football,
rain before nosing about my father's rusting tools

his vice, scattered screws. Recently, I souvenired
his Driza-Bone—torn, faded, the coat he wore ploughing,
to get cows and calves in. I look to its smells
of paddocks, tractors, his way of thinking
hanging from a nail in my garage.

My mother's hands rarely form a fist. They are open
to washing dishes, making cups of tea
each simple action becomes a prayerful routine.
What follows after breakfast—light through
kitchen venetians, talkback railing
from a football radio. I watch her lift
glad wrap from a salad, settle for cold meat
from yesterday's leg of ham. This is why
I drive two hours between lockdowns, just to watch her
relaying news of check-ups, who she ran into while shopping
a kitchen table, the only distance between us.

# What I return to and miss

Like random thoughts of the coming week
white cockatoos rise and fall over a paddock of stones.
Out here on the Foxhow Road where the mind is let go
the dip and curve of their scurrying flight
blends with the memories I rely upon for argument.

A single strand electric fence enables Black Polls
to feed beside the road. Next to the cows, a line
of wooden posts recedes into a shallow lake.
This is horizontal country where what I bury
rises to the surface along ribbons of bitumen
with the sun in my eyes.

Crumbling stonewall fences
sacred dwelling sites, stories I haven't heard
isolated roads I drive to be found in.
Townships diminish, dusky salt pans endure
yet like the certainty of a doubt Mt Elephant
manages to hold the paddocks down.

I pull over, take a photo, spear grass whispers in a breeze.
A lone car barrels out of a bend. This is what I know—
this channelled longing, inescapable as a blaze of canola
spreading down to a gunmetal lake.
Yet knowledge is more than absorbing these back roads
or noticing sheep standing on a dam bank's mound.

It's the questions that surface with each escape
from lockdown. The passing view of Mount Myrtoon—
in Djargurd Wurrung country, a low-slung scoria cone
fenced into a paddock, fenced into silences.

I keep looking back to five wind-slanted cypresses
on a distant ridge, the spaces between them confirm
what it is I return to and miss.

# Caravan

Each time I return to the highway
a caravan in a paddock decays a little further.
An eight-berther, upended, slanted on bricks
its door removed, I glimpse the shadowy recesses
of someone's life from a previous century.

Parked beside some cypress trees
it's one of the many ruins I see rusting in paddocks,
testament to lives halted by a Volkswagen or Datsun
capeweed reclaiming a Commodore.

Each ruin becomes a road sign
for how far it is I have to drive
markers to the years
the way fallen branches wreathe a dead tree,
paint peeling from the van's sides
like the skin on a farmer's nose
a wife notices.

# A tin kettling

They wander across paddocks banging saucepans.
Neighbours, family, kids who can clatter a pot
ambling through summer light after milking.
Cut paddocks, quiet gravel roads, the prospect of Christmas
in a town that goes to Mass on a Saturday night.

Like saying the rosary, they walk into ritual
led by what's expected—catching out a couple
still getting used to being hitched.
This makeshift orchestra of grins and kettles
banging, tapping, hoohah shouting

drawing the newly-weds out from a porch.
*You buggers have got a cheek.*
*Get inside for something to eat.*
Saucepans laid down with shoes by the door
anybody who can has called in to postpone

their quiet nights together. Long necks are uncapped
children stand around not knowing
where to look. Two saucepan lids crash
a violin is struck. The talk that two people make
rises unsteady as smoke beside towering cypress trees.

# The potato bag needle

Piercing the hessian, pulling the baling twine through
loose cross-stitch, quick tug of the seam
straightening with the knee, another bag
propped in a crooked line by the furrows.

Scooping up potatoes in dark volcanic soil
dirt in my fingernails, dust up my nose.
Stooping and shuffling forward, my future
owned by the stories of picking my father told.

Some pickers could line up 180 bags in a day
I didn't last a week waiting for the semi-trailer
to roll in, eighteen wheels flattening my dreams.
Pick and sew, pick and sew, load up, pick and sew.

I grabbed one end of a bag, a local held
the other. In one fluid motion we swung
each bag onto the tray, above our heads, three high.
The driver guiding each sack with a metal hook

into place, the same hook he might have used
hay-carting. He shoved them, kneed them into rows
before tying the hitch knots I could never master.
Legs jellied, I stumbled around

lifted by the kind of work my father dreams of
propped up in his electric lift chair watching the races
the job ahead of him. He knows
he'll never scoop the black soil of Crossley again.

A rusted curved needle rests on my window sill
copper baling twine threaded as if it could still be used
like a story we no longer need. To love is to believe
in this bent ornament that once passed through hessian.

# Mostly

Saturdays, weeding between brick pavers
in the shade of a wonky trellis
roar of an MCG crowd coming at me in waves.
Trains clattering past, silver through the trees.
Sometimes I read the poets, catch an oblong of sky
but mostly I am stirred by the hum of Hoddle Street
a constant murmur like the ocean
on a windy night.

Mostly, our neighbours trim over-hanging
branches, throw them back over the fence
watch our bins, ask about work, babies,
air their rugs over front fences.

They know the street is a car width wide
who lives at numbers 17, 42 and 35, who
they have to speak English with. I nearly cried
watching their cousin being hauled into a Divvy van.
He'd been handing over plastic bags to passing cars
for weeks.

Mostly, we watch the street from the safety
of bull nose verandahs, straining to glimpse
a hallway, each of us striving for something
out of reach like a train flashing through a puddle.

Each night our neighbours sit on their concrete verandah
catching passersby from around five—cousins, mothers,
old men in cardigans. Later, within the darkened glow
of a streetlight they fall quiet, an open front door between them.

# Hanging out the washing

Sometimes you just need to hang out the washing
lose yourself beneath a Hills Hoist, meet the needs
of the next hour pegging along the seams, forgetting
about words, seek out familiar smells of damp cotton
crumpled folds of jeans, nylon blouses that rustle over fingers.

Sometimes I end up staring at a brick wall
adrift in the moment of shaking creases from a tee-shirt
with the random thoughts standing under a clothes-line gives.
I watched my mother jiggle a basket between five clothes lines
each line propped by a sapling with a knotty forked end—
shirts, trousers and nighties billowing to the smells
of cowyard and machinery shed

Whenever there is a need to give your self over to the peg bag
let the wind do its work on sheets and towels
carry the voices of friends who have died
friends you are not ready to eulogize
peg out a shirt whenever there is a gap on the line.

# Self-seeded

The gum tree on the farm across the road
older than I am, present all my life, is
starting to drop its branches.
From the top of a passing trailer load of hay
I have brushed its leaves
I have photographed the curve and sway
of its upper limbs, the way it commands
flat, dry paddocks, cloudless blue sky.
I have rubbed its bark, stood under it in drizzling rain
watched rusting farm machinery accumulate
beneath its shade. Beside this Sugar Gum, a shit-
splattered gravel lane leads to a paddock space
that housed the neighbour's peeling weatherboard.
Yet the tree, self-seeded as I am, remains
utterly free where I stand before it
with my questions.

# Signatures

# Wimmera light

Cropping paddocks stretch on
a lone car encounters a gravel road
away from the highway.
Graffiti on a signal box outside Pimpinio
vast skies, ominous clouds shadow
the isolation within. Ghostly turn
of wind turbines on a ridge.
Released from lockdown, here the light threatens
as if the city never mattered.

# The Stick Shed of Murtoa

We wander into darkness by a side entrance
someone's bike leans against a wall. It is the hush
that greets me, of people lowering their voices in a cathedral.
Rectangles of light stretch in perspective along the roof.
Lines of mountain ash poles recede into shadow.
Steel cables anchor the poles like in an Escher sketch.
Between each line of poles is an avenue
of concrete, scrubbed as the flagstones of Notre-Dame.
I walk between rows of unmilled poles subdued
by what people could build in 1941–
a tin shed 265 metres in length, monument
to working lives beside silo and rail line.
An older man leans back with his phone
to capture the height, the way the poles rise
as sentinels to the roof's darkened trusses.
Next it's a selfie with his mates
grinning up into the light, shaking their heads
at what an empty grain shed can make you do.

# Wimmera junk

Corrugated iron house
shells of Holden utes parked in a weedy back yard
patched-up weatherboards, gas bottles by the side
rusted water tanks, a collection of bike statues
across a front yard.

Over a strand of wire
a threatening sea of wheat
stretching toward the ruin of a shearing shed.

Here are dimensions of punishing light
the old argument to live is to drive
even to stand, is to feel eyes behind curtains
gaps lingering between your words
silences of the Recreation Reserve.

Here are ways to be trapped
by a brown sheet hanging over the window
of the former Uniting church,
as if there has always been horizontals
to stare at, the distant grumble of B-doubles
pummelling through from Adelaide.

# Driving through mallee towns

Straight roads give you time to think
watch wheat fields unroll. Here you know
where the horizon stands: far-off, remembered
the light unrelenting as a migraine coming on.

Behind a row of houses facing main street
is the scrub, Mallee stumps, dry creek bed.
A high school clings to a view of canola crops
the need to escape appears to be generational.

Red brick two-storey hotels closed down
op shops thriving on a street that could be
a stage set. In the hardware store, a line
of rifles, cross-bows on shelves, but the threat

is in the flatness you never knew
a mirage distorting the road ahead.
You focus by holding onto the wheel
driven to flee from where thoughts have led

## Bleached paddocks

Driving light of harvested paddocks
light that lifts you, transcends the stubble
dust billowing from headers, a narrow lane
leading to three wheat silos. The skies
are endless or brooding, clouds thickening
from the west. The Hamilton highway bisects
this dreaming of paddocks that stretch
to the white blades of a wind farm,
clusters of round bales sloping about
an empty lake. Summer's heat rises
with the dust and blonde seed heads bursting
along gravel lanes. On windless afternoons
my energies are thwacked, drawn
to the light bleached by childhood walks
to the river, tussocks and rye grass brushing
my shins, thighs, grass dust and seeds
clogging the air. Little did I know that by
emptying the paddocks of hay bales, I would be
returning to the passing light all these years later.
Burnouts etched into narrow back roads, lines
of tyre tread visible on the bitumen.
It's become a thing to decorate round bales
dress them up as Santa for traffic passing the stubble.
Something timeless in these signs, these burnouts
how the paddocks either dry or bake, memories
frizzled by light in late December. Beyond the road kill
galahs and cockatoos lift and screech, the light
more than nostalgia, shimmers.

# Language of rubs

Uphill, the Friesians are feeding
from trails of silage; bunching up
flicking tails that have been lopped

to a two-foot stem. Music
of their eating, snorting,
sideways grind of a jaw

chewing as they walk
from trail to trail like people
browsing between stalls at a market—

interested, preoccupied, distracted by flies
flicking strands of hay onto their backs
drowsing the itchy spots.

They file off toward a corrugated iron water trough
nodding, rubbing up against a neck
nuzzle of head against head

older cows bullying a heifer back
a language of rubs
I can only guess at.

# A taste for blood

rattle of a dog chain on corrugated iron
ratchetty notes from the tank he slept in

hauling a sheep's carcass by rope over a cypress branch
watching it dangle, after milking
smell of blood-stained body bag
satisfied, there'd be meat tomorrow

neighbour said it was your dog again
neighbour could turn a game of footy on his boot

the gouged necks, back legs missing, the mess
of blood-matted wool crows flocked to

Bluey didn't roam, he liked to nip
a Friesian's ankles, gnaw at sheep's gizzards

down by the drain. I've drowned kittens
knocked calves on the head, tasted
blood spurting from a killer's neck

watching a dead sheep swing was no crime
looping the chain over a cypress limb
pulling until Bluey was yelping
wriggling, wild-eyed dancing until
I tied off, walked over to the machinery shed
where the crow bars and shovels were cold to touch

nobody need know when the squeal of a dog halts
I started feeding milk to the calves
the only thing a farmer could do
once a dog has a taste for blood

next day, neighbour called round
lambs had been chased down, taken
by one of his own

# Between the pen and the roundabout

Ear-tagged, matted coats drenched by rain
two dead Friesian calves and a near-dead Guernsey
dumped on the roundabout like soldiers left in the mud
in a Netflix documentary.

Three metres from the corpses, two pens of Friesian calves
undercover, hopping in ankle-deep sawdust, ambling up
to suck at my fingers. Each calf is ear-tagged to an A.I bull—
*Altamatt, Karma.*

Beside the heifers a pen of bull calves
stare into the middle-distance, brooding
as if they know they are about to be turned into steers
by the tightening constriction of a rubber ring.

Between the pen and the roundabout
is a muddy patch of gravel tractors and utes
idle over. A space to watch a cow
returning to the dairy to moan for a lost calf,

a space between the living and the dead
measured by the rise and fall of the near-dead calf's
matted coat, a space where I'm owned by the need to look away.
*It's not often you get three buggers dead in the morning.*

# A squeeze of paddocks

Every weed is a memory, a slanted hayshed
bends time. Casuarinas droop and sway
somebody is moping in the right lane.
You glance at the paddocks remember
the buzz of crickets, locusts flicking over
cracked ground, flung twigs
the wobbling horizon.

Late afternoon light is beckoning you to rise
out of the driver's seat
for a moment to elevate, be transcendent
hovering above the road in your shorts
and tee shirt, lifting off

the way the chords of a favourite song
transcend places, decades, except here
it is a glimpse of lemony bitten-down paddocks
giving the kick, lifting you above

tail-gating SUVs, a roundabout, Bunnings—
announcing the next town. This is where
loss will take you. A squeeze of paddocks—
the country you will pass back into.

# Mushrooms

Like thistles, they spread and congregate
wherever a spore is cast. Blue caps, Buttercups

insistent as capeweed after an early break
they are said to talk to each other

the way memories do, converging
like cattle tracks before a gateway.

A network of signals dispersing
across paddocks the way family talk

continued after Mass, after lunch.
 Our mushrooms *did not inherit the earth*

but added flavour to mashed potatoes.
Fried or stewed, pungent as fresh eels scooped

from Mt Emu Creek, Mum dished them up
on toast, until like all changes, the sprinkling

of white on slopes and ridges became an absence
a death that was gradual, quietly accepted.

Fertilized paddocks, heavy in phosphate
kept cows in production, mushrooms silent.

# Between a paddock and a hayshed

The longing begins
  when washing dishes,
places you are called back to
  in the supermarket car park
waiting at a roundabout
  walking out of a fruit grocer
into late afternoon light, places
  that buffet, wash through you
the way a memory scrapes at a residue.

I remember the groan and sway of a trailer
  130 bales stacked and bound.
Rocking to the rhythms of the load
  fumes from the tractor lulling
my brother and I into a stasis—
  ten minutes nodding off to the lean of the axle
floorboards of the trailer
  creaking like old doors opening,
a daydreaming head-lolling space
  the trailer rolling through shallow
grassy drains, hay bales shifting their weight.

From on top, I counted the paddocks on our farm
  ran my eye along the boundary fence,
training myself to read distances—
  those blurred, extended feelings between fence posts.
But mostly, I was clutching at the leaves of passing gum trees
  looking to the treeless hump of a mountain
to see what could become of my brother and I
  sleeping on the job
between a paddock and a hayshed.

# The flattened grass patches

The flattened grass patches
where cows have lain from the night before
remind me how close they were to each other,
how they depended upon proximity and
intimacy for warmth, their odorous
grassy breaths, their heavy breathing
audible in the darkness metres away.
There was always one or more cows standing
sentry-like, while the rest of the herd sat
staring, chewing, their dark eyes glowing
under starless skies.

These impressions the cows leave behind
remind me of how people fell in Pompei
their bodies imprinted in ash, preserved
the way memory encases the heat
from where cows have lain,
a heat that lingers the way a circle
of cowshed shows where they rose to regard dawn
breaking over Moloney's silage bales.

# Undertow

It's Anzac Day and the country is asleep.
Somebody has welded a magpie to a letter box.
It throws me, momentarily, as the small gatherings
in towns along the Western Plains.

A student sitting in class asks
*what is the war on terror?*
Wikipedia provides links to Bin Laden
Al Qaeda, Bush, September 11

yet there isn't a clear explanation.
*The neutrality of the article is disputed.*
Jean Duverney founded Cressy in 1837
this much can also be disputed.

A display map nailed to the toilet block wall
urges me to discover the Western Plains.
I remember the newspaper sub-headings—
'war on terror', each page apportioning blame

still, the Woady Yaloak inches between reeds.
Around a sweeping bend, stands of eucalypts
lean in. After days of relentless newspaper saturation
it comes down to this—wreaths arrayed

around cenotaphs, a circle of men
nursing stubbies outside a fire-station
flags half-mast front of weatherboard halls.
Modest ceremonies for the men who jumped

to enlist, to escape, their names chiselled into stone
remnants of an attitude, a value, a community
yet the paddocks were always a memory field—
Fighting Waterholes, Murdering Gully,

car wrecks piled up behind farmhouses
*Metricon* homes plonked in treeless bogs.
The student will make up something about terrorism.
It will become an attitude.

# Signatures

I'm walking down a cattle track into paddock quiet

the reach of tree shadows extending
like my mother's voice calling to get out of bed.
Baling twine snagged on a barbed wire fence

kangaroos watching me from the back paddocks.
Dry, cracked, hoof-pocked earth around drains
spider webs strung between fence wires.

Another season wrapped in silage bales
mist rising off the mountain to the tune
of a crow symphony. A rusted water tank

resting on weathered sleepers, a clump
of eucalypts I expect to always be there, along
with the dumped ploughs and stained bath tubs

every where I look there are signatures to this land.

# Drive

Once a year I take a drive to the gravel
twists and turns of a back road
descending into clefts and valleys
past cypress-shadowed weatherboards
fibro houses, Rabbit Control signs.

───────────────

My hands feathering the wheel
the land rising and falling
into a left-hander where once I slowed
to watch a tiger snake ripple across the corrugations
bush silence that is immersive as ferns
 acacias, stone wall fences, saplings
twisting out of rock, their branches gnarled
as if frozen.

───────────────

I follow the road's humps—
a state of mind that appears untouched
since colonial times. I don't know where
I'm being driven to, but know it is not
a place I'd rather remain.
Paddocks of stone, Friesian heifers
up at the fence line in drizzling rain
I drive to return to what takes me away.

Taking it slow

# Park life

They sit around camp-fires in ugg boots
nursing a stubby, sometimes a grandchild.
They watch the new arrivals closely
studying the reversing methodology.
Left hand down, right hand down
camp trailer arcing toward an annexe
engine revving, trailer jackknifing.
*If only, you'd listen to me!*

———————————

A twelve-month old baby latches onto the hip
of her father while he packs up their campervan
dumping bags, shoes, coats and guy ropes in a heap.
Stooping to unwind the roof, he hands the baby
to her mother. The baby's legs form the shape
of latching-on, mid-air, as though the baby knew
what to expect as the mother did, a reflex act.

———————————

The topless man with the Moses beard has been drinking
with the neighbours all afternoon
sitting round a burner out front of their *Jayco*
a boom-box
cranked to 80s hits, Harley and ute beside him.
He doesn't wear a mask
his passing looks have the blunt landings of conspiracy theories.
At two am
he is hollering against the virus, lies of the Premier
swearing to peacocks and crows.

———————————

Unable to sleep
my wife and I tip-toe in slippers over gravel
eyes averted
flames snapping above his burner, u.v light spotlighting
his circling voice.
There's an edge to his rants I might have confronted in my dreams
but for now
I wait under a park light outside the toilets for something
to be unleashed.

───────────────

Sitting on the deck of a make-shift shack a man listens
to Patsy Cline.
Her velvet notes gliding over pre-fab huts, over peacocks
fluttering onto roofs
or stepping lightly through camp-sites, their multi-coloured tails held aloft
like gifts behind them.
Earlier, he had been tinkering under the bonnet of his *Camira*
soaping the quarter panels
with bucket and sponge settling into a suburban groove of ownership, pride.
Now he sits alone on a green plastic chair considering
the gum trees with a can.

───────────────

A toddler holds onto a guy rope,
walks around it in circles, falls
to the ground giddy, laughing.
She plays this game again and again
while her parents fold in the beds
of their campervan. I walk past
a circle of chairs and laughter
remembering how I learnt to back
a two-wheel trailer under the eye
of my father, noting what it meant
to be a certain type of man.

───────────────

I've always tried to rush my family into schedules
of lining up bags
by the front door, firing off questions, with each passing deadline
I lost track of words.
Single-minded, I was out the door waiting
like my father
blowing the car horn at my mother, putting on her shoes, rushing to turn off
an oven before Mass.
Typically, I manage to isolate myself into a furball of energy
wound-up
pacing around loaded shopping bags
adopting
the faltering belligerent stance I recognised in men about me.

———————————

Over time, I found myself adrift in the quiet of caravan parks
after people
had left for morning routines, visiting sites or going for the walks
I might get to after the next cup of tea.
Sometimes I'd look up to the slow sway of a stringy bark canopy
allow memories to surface then float.
Sometimes I drifted through a day shifting a camp chair, chasing the warmth
of a teasing, indifferent sun.

## Petrichor

Between late summer rains
we leave gurgling down-pipes
for an ice cream in the city.

Clouds are amassing
smells of lawn, memory and mulch
a sense of flux, of evening swirl.

Bats are flying west, roads glisten
we finish each other's sentences
our talk swept along by family jokes

foggy car windows, the prospect
of scooping Rum n Raisin on a flimsy footpath table
smells of the city bubbling around us.

# Waiting for my daughter to finish work

Faded paling fence, bitumen footpath
    row of single-storey red brick units visible above the fence line.
An empty car park except for a disposable blue mask.
    Antennas, verticals of light towers rising over trees.
What I am thinking is beneath me—those other nights
    waiting for clubs and training to finish
        concentrated views
of an oval between trees, a grey brick wall,
    kitchen hands smoking by an exit door
        parents in cars
on their phones, some fanning the air-con.

I look and scroll to the view I spend time in
        am confronted by
a suburban street receding down hill
    lichen on dark tiles, the backyard fence that has become
        another altar I return to.

Across the city, people are waiting before shutters, brick walls
    or in the shade of a plane tree. Some of them are cursing
their turn to do pick-up, some of them are circling
        moving over land as in a dream
some of them are caught by the repeating lines
    of a paling fence and the beauty of waiting.

# She plugs in

to the light of The Cocteau Twins
layers of voice to escape to
storylines to insert herself in.
I edge onto the main road
neither of us speak, comfortable
in our glances at passing houses
cocoon of familiar front gardens.
Something visceral transports us
beyond the first hill.
The Breeders, Neil Young, Jesus
and Mary Chain distribute my longing.
Hijacked by memories, each traffic light
allows me to recede—
the morning of her birth, dress-ups.
She applies lip balm, foundation
parts her fringe in the visor mirror
works through her phone.
Already I have missed whatever
transcends her dreams.
I plant it up the Shannon Road hill
both of us tired, reluctant, listing
classes to avoid in our heads.
For it is music that compels us
to quietly resist the world
of the ten minute commute.
Cars stream towards us
a lollipop man ventures onto the road.
I'm banking on a green arrow
she is tapping playlists, talking
without any need for words.

# I do this, I do that

Preparing breakfast for the girls, dressing them, making up L's lunch for kinder—cheese sandwiches, an orange, carrot sticks, crackers, a fruit cup that she won't eat, kissing A goodbye at 7am, cramming in my own breakfast while I glance over the newspaper headlines and if it is quiet, quickly read an article that appeals, gather the kinder bag, drop L off at kinder then drive to Drysdale to the Safeway for the house grocery shopping, return home, unpack groceries, prepare R's lunch, drive off to pick up the Toy Library key from Jan and do Toy Library duty from 11-12pm with R easily entertained by the toys yet she is falling asleep as I drive home, keep her awake long enough to swallow some sandwiches and put her to bed. I have two hours off, well sort of. I eat lunch, organize a load of washing, do an hour's weeding in the front garden, look at some poems, decide that I'm happy with them, pick R up and drive off to collect L at 2:45, return home, unpack her bag, start the girls off playing outside on the swing and in the sandpit, hang out the washing, walk up to Catherine's with the girls for afternoon tea, an hour later return home, make the girls rock melon snacks while I prepare dinner and they watch a video. We eat dinner, but the girls are crying missing their mummy. After dinner, I bath them and then begin preparing their warm cups of milk before bed when A arrives home at 7:30pm and takes over the reading of books. I wash the dishes, tidy up the kitchen and then after the girls are in bed we catch up with our days at 8:45pm. I insist on a whiskey before Denton.

# The ineffable

On a good day the beach was a smell away
I was tracing footpaths in search of a city

a cat on a window ledge
The Clash blaring from an open window.

I passed young drunks weaving in daylight
an old woman pushing her shopping trolley of bags and clothes

punters looking sideways before they stepped outside a TAB
dodgy men at a bus stop sizing up potential threats

two greasy take-aways I knew were good for selling Dim Sims.
At night their red neon signs renewed another era

where women stood on street corners
deals passing between palms in daylight.

I have always been drawn to the order and chaos of Op shops
faded Oils high above racks of shoes, stuffed toys, stacked glassware.

I have always wanted to be taken out of myself, lost
to a world of browsing, searching for the ineffable

amongst Joyce Cary, Camus, Len Deighton.
I knew I was compelled to keep looking

on a street of rooming houses, crawling police cars
syringes in gutters, stained footpaths.

I was a country boy who had ventured north
I had to keep my wits about me.

# The explosion

Too nervous to socialize with housemates
I sang and danced with my door closed
to *Cuyahoga*. Once I cranked up Ride

before going out with an unsure friend.
It was like being dropped off by a harried parent—
we smiled, looked away, looked again.

The music that enters me does so
when I'm alone, driving, waking
overheard music alters the day—

a neighbour in the flat above, his footsteps
creaking overhead each night
*Yellow Submarine* on repeat after work.

I need music to take me out of myself
a chorus, a guitar riff that can lift me to the ceiling
like when a singer turns the mike back to the crowd

notes and chords move to blossom about me
like an amp beginning to fizz, in such moments
it seems that I could open up and explode.

# Skinheads

I know what it is like to be marked
by a nervousness before waves, a reluctance
to act like a dickhead in front of friends.
My male role models were hard-working, crease-
necked men who threw their hat on the floor
waited for tea to be served to them.
The codes of behaviour for men were unwritten
and fiercely upheld. Men chased sons with stockwhips
slept with a gun under the bed, drank in isolated
bush shacks. Any woman who lived alone
in a country farmhouse was on watch.
It was within this environment that I began
to read all I could about skinheads.

# What we did to each other

I used to catch him on my way to the tram stop
sitting out front of his weatherboard in shorts
wheelchair parked on a concrete path.
There were clouds dissolving over the Bay
container ships stationery on the horizon.
He wasn't going far, just across the tram tracks
to drink with locals sitting on stools, smoking
their voices crackling and spitting from throat cancer.
At the time, my job as a sawyer had me on the lookout
for stacks of timber swinging through the air
sometimes at head height. Customer orders
of cut oregon and pine were hoisted by strap
and crane over the bread and butter rows
of eight be twos, eight be threes and ten be twos.
The stamped numbers of 8:25, 8:21 and 5:03
recorded my days as did folded notes
in a manila pay envelope. There was a simple beauty
to stuffing notes into my jean's front pocket
of never being short, unlike the email
on pay week today with its list of numbers
that can't be counted between your fingers.
Each lunch I bought a hamburger and sav in batter
hoping to catch the eye of women in greasy
take-aways skimming eggs from hot fryers
their eyes dulled by steam and scribbled orders.
The timber yard collected itinerants from sawmills
around Jamieson and Yarra Glen.
An old Croatian arrived with a Gladstone bag
sat on wooden benches alone in the staff room
watching me get whipped in table-tennis each lunch time.
His English was faltering but he had the strength
needed in a tight situation. Each day was a repeat

of tailing out—sliding a cut length of timber
back at the sawyer for it to be cut down again.
One day a length of timber became stuck
in the bandsaw, was let loose at such a speed
the person tailing out was sent flying
back into the wall of the office, a length of timber
impaled in his stomach. After work drinks—
were obligatory as a bedrock of tall stories and unreliable men
who might turn up stoned, hungover or want to fight you.

But not Vinny Meade. He walked back and forward
into his life for eight hours along the sawdust-
sprinkled tracks. I recruited him from the country
hoping he would give into the screech of the bandsaw
sliding eight be threes back at me with a smirk and a ciggie
until it all became a floating dream—sawdust
clouding the air, eyes lifting to a round silver clock.
I learnt how to defeat a man by keeping him on track.
Both of us were like Sisyphus, absorbed by routine
going nowhere and running out of things to say to each other.
He returned to the cows, died too young. I didn't measure up.

Truths and exaggerations were part of the air
I breathed in Port Melbourne. The Painters and Dockers
were always looked after, their orders
rushed through for free.
Most workers were missing forefingers or thumbs.
A rollie helped some people lift something greater than themselves.
One day a saw sharpener was fixing a problem
at the bandsaw. I swung a flitch from a stack
bounced it on a wooden trolley, guided it toward
the bandsaw that buzzed and jiggered
like something uncontained. It was a job
I performed each day, catching a rhythm
with the flitches, balancing thirty feet of oregon on a trolley
pointing its breadth toward a humming blade.

Something waylaid the sharpener.
I bounced the flitch onto the trolley
but couldn't contain the force of its swing.
The flitch slid to the floor trapping the sharpener's
ankle against the steel trolley rails. His cry of pain
let me know the ankle was smashed. We pulled
the flitch away. He was sixty and never worked again.
I escaped the timber yard with my fingers and the dream
of trying to catch the flitch before it crushed his ankle.
What we did to each other and learnt to look away from
made those days bearable or necessary
as the man in the wheelchair pushing himself
across the tram tracks towards his obligations.

# Taking it Slow

My great-grandfather liked to take things slowly
trailing the cows he bought in Terang back to Warrnambool—
   a distance of 45 kms, all the while walking with his hands
clasped behind his back in the early part of the twentieth century
   a man who fondled potatoes, rosary beads, was noted
in a newspaper obituary.
   My brother and I learned to take it slow walking behind 120 Jerseys
along a back road of ferns and stringybarks, catching their big-boned swaying rhythm
   looking for a dawdling calm, following the leader
into bush country that had mostly been cleared.
   In time, my brother and I came to know the curves and ridges of this road—
when to expect rabbits or an echidna bunched in the gravel.
   We drove the cows 15 ks to Swan's Lane for summer feed, autumn
we walked them back, heavily pregnant, pausing uphill
      from Brucknell Creek where the bitumen rises then drops, our futures
mapped by a herd that was ready to calve.
   Each morning I like to take things slow—
release the pup from her crate, clean her mess
   wipe down the black plastic floor mat.
Each action driven by cause and effect
   following her out the sliding door, across the deck
down the concrete ramp to the back lawn.
   She squats beside an apple tree, a routine that wakes me.
I pour pellets into her silver metal bowl, make coffee
   stroke her back while she sniffs under the chair
I think of my great-grandfather
   walking from Warrnambool to Ararat
to visit his daughter in the *lunatic* asylum. The kind of random thoughts
   I followed sliding blocks of cheese along a conveyor belt—
tracing a pattern with my hands while thinking about something else.
   Twice a year my great-grandfather tramped through bush
skirted the Hopkins, shifted through Hexham, Willaura

to pay the fees for his *highly strung daughter*
one of many teenagers, housewives, women enduring mania
   of polite disposition, captured in grainy black and whites.
Insignificant, history-less women locked behind peep hole doors
   suddenly visible all these years later through stories I cannot trust.
Where was my great-grandfather taken on those walks to Ararat?
   Losing himself amongst the ferns, the way my brother and I mumbled
to each other, scuffing our rubber boots along gravel and bitumen
   my great-grandfather taking it slow along dirt tracks, his daughter, Minnie,
on laundry or kitchen duty for years, a woman who couldn't look after herself
   dependent on routine to wake her in the scrubbed linoleum wards.
I spoon some peanut butter into a Kong for the pup
   her restless energies, focused, calmed as the morning can ever be.

# Hurt

In the video for Cash's cover of *Hurt*
Trent Reznor's words bear the weight of parable.
Cash's washed-out, swollen face cannot hide
the stare of intent, the look that is itself
an evaluation. It is a song of questions
his voice a gravel road.
Seated at a table of rotting fruit
champagne, lobster, close-up eye of dead fish
Cash pours red wine over his *Last Supper*
consecrating his pills, his jailhouse odes, his wife
June, looking on with the concern of a God.
Here is Cash, charismatic outsider, bereft and alone.
A montage splices a life, the piano repeats like a person
shaking a knee—grinning father at the wheel of a train
pensive, walking along a beach, peering in
to the abandoned family home.
A shutter speed of images you might see before you die
symbols you are left to wear
 a life you have learnt to train a stare against.

# Dirt

Rollo's Road narrows to the heavy strum
of a bass string
Cash's gravelly voice fits the memories
I chase.
A cattle track view of a sugar gum
older than my mother's smile for
Cliff Portwood.
Am I obsessive, driven to measure
the spaces between lone trees?
I keep returning to the pull
of Nirranda, Nullawarre, Naringal
farmers stuttering on local hall stages
towering cypress hedges, tanker mud
around dairies.
I take wrong turns, reverse back over
what I thought could be trusted.
I can belong somewhere
hurtling along the Cobden Warrnambool Road
past roadside weeds, pockets of bush,
alone, never still as the dreams that wake me.

# Arumpo Road

you hit the bitumen and meet a death
of tyres on loose gravel
rattles in the front guard, stones flicking up
eyes focused on the clay patches

a road that soaks up rains, kicks up dust
entwines tyre marks in mud
a road that moves through time

distorting memories, unsettling
my outsider view with its judder of corrugations
clay pans and the wandering mind

where twisted Mallee trunks give way to stretches of saltbush
a fence line of iron droppers intrudes
disconnected, I'm listening to tyres on gravel again

water from recent rains pools in the middle of the road
bullet holes in a faded sign, a family of goats trot into scrub
the road is a crease in red sand, a back story

of what I thought I knew of country
white gravel on pink clay
clouds of dust blossoming over the road

we wave to oncoming drivers
on bitumen we don't
compacted gravel pock-marked like a weathered face
our talk falls away

where the sky drops to the horizon
this road is haunted by roll-overs
spin-outs, bogged SUVs
a stubby rests on a 44 gallon drum

this road is an umbilical cord pulling
us with magnetic force to bone fragments
darkened clay of stone ovens
women's footprints dancing in the sand

# Lament

# All her glories

Heavy as stone, we wrap her in an old white sheet
carry her along the pavers to the back yard steps
all her glories—her wet nose against my leg, scratch
marks on doors, her nudging for a pat, swiping slices
from a plate, trotting out the back, a loaf of bread
between her jaws, the pacing at 5pm, dancing in circles
to be fed, her excitement at the beach, running over sand
plunging into water paddling back to shake her black coat
next to us before jumping into the water again.

We carry these with us.

Rolling over grass, rubbing up against a retaining wall
her tongue drooling in the car, her long drinks at a blue bucket
pulling on her leash, walking from side to side in front of us
rearing up at any dog, a guinea pig in her jaws, snarling
at a terrier on its back below her, brown feathers of four chooks
scattered across the yard, the wire gate she rammed a hole through.
Leaping for a ball, flying down steps, carrying her Kong
like a prize then dropping it amongst some weeds, the bones
she buried in the vegie patch, sitting up in the driver's seat
until we returned from the shops.

We carry these with us.

We heard the howl on a Tuesday night, saw
the line she had crossed over, despite her swollen
stomach, weak heart she paced around us with a grin
the dog flap shuddered behind her.
We hugged and cried around her snoozing on the hospital rug
one of us wept over Facetime for the goodest dog
her front leg shaved, this centre of our lives

drawing hands and faces to her grey nose.
Nearly seventeen, we lower her into a hole in the back yard
read poems and letters before dropping them in.
We pour dirt onto the white sheet but fail to let go
she that has run around our back yard so much
we are shoveling dirt onto her.
She is beneath, under, below, somewhere within.
 We walk into the kitchen waiting for the scrape
of her paws on the floorboards.

# Tell it

The music of her key in the security door
the latch switched back
first eyes, a kiss, a cheek
bags dumped, scarf unwound
she slides over to cradle a daughter
moon over a cat on the arm rest.

First wines, crackers and dip
paused by the nightly two minutes of hate—
hit n runs, court trials, machete attacks.
Hummous devoured, a text returned
we bring home the work they say you should never do.
No names, just moments to be explained
behaviours we deplore in people
looking out for themselves
skivving off, a work mate's cackle
we need to get out of our heads.

Outside in the dimming light
house lights flick at the valley's darkness.
We drain our wines listening
without judgement to one other person
in the world who gets it
each time and totally there while the rice cooker bubbles
because work gives a day reason to bring it back home and tell it
the next night and the next night again.

# You

Echiums are on the rise, blue cones spiking winter air
you organise a sick daughter texting on the kitchen bench.

The Jacaranda refuses to flower, our apples are peppered by Black Spot
all you need is a free morning to write through.

The salvias droop and sway their purple wands
you rev up the girls with Dickens and a hug.

Proteas catch your eye, you make a vow to root out oxalis
portioning dinners for your mother, thermos of tea on the run.

The Blue Pacific is expanding, there are shrubs you avoid
my mistakes with lawn, your suggestions from the deck.

Daphne fragrances adrift at the front door, the maple shedding its leaves
our money falls then rises like a pot dependent on seasonal rain.

The weeds, the ivy, the neighbour's house flattened to a sub-division block
friendships you bend with a text, pull taut with a call.

Your bench load of cuttings striking out in the laundry
the way you pause to hold the limp of a dog.

# True

Enduring silences by the side of the house
shadowy spread of a callistemon, spectre
of hydrangeas I hacked out with an axe
a sleeping child on the cusp

of your shoulder, another daughter
dragging the nappy bag.
Coming home to a feeble light over the deck
memories like an outward sigh we share
dog eyes find us fumbling with a sliding
door lock, carrying the voices of parents
the way they gave into first things.
We take a clear path to the kettle, toilet
flushed cheeks of a daughter being folded
into bed.

What remains of the backyard I followed with a hose?
The view was in my head — row of birch saplings
espaliered apple, ingrained, smelt, touched
like tracing a finger along your arm
or closing my eyes to the loop of back roads
leading home.

I was learning to improvise with lavender under the clothesline
a setting for tea cups and plastic biscuits in a cubby house
pelicans circling like birthday gatherings on the lawn.
I fell into days that became a pause
watching a daughter learn to walk.

Late afternoon flutters through the Silver Princess
A pony club paddock gives me bearings from a church pew.
Views from a verandah, occasional waft of gravel dust
my thinking stretched by what I imagine to be true.

# Anniversary Poem

Looking up into the canopy of a white-
limbed gum tree
cloudless blue behind
lawnmower in the distance
crows, shrieks of cockatoos
swooping and gliding to
leaves and foliage spilling
towards you
like a rush of memories
unbidden with all the birds of the Central Goldfields
singing late afternoon calls—
do-whops and bells, the silences in between
light from the hills falling through
branches and you are looking up
with the focus of a child
checking out the droop of leaves, slender
lines of a white trunk the
windless afternoon extending extending.

# At the lake's edge

A ripple falls against mudflats
we look to the hump of a mountain range
someone is fishing from a green kayak
a woman sits cross-legged on a boat ramp, waiting.

I follow your thoughts to the middle-distance
where the surface is dark, hard, a sheen
we pause before fish scraps and shale
listening to the endless slump and pull of water

and further off, the dip and drag of the kayaker's oar.
Unsurprisingly, the lake is down on other years
leaving a pale wrack line of tide marks etched
like our pasts on mossy rocks.

Moving to the country could be a place
to be calm, creative, released from lattes
and tradies in over-sized utes. A breeze falters
I return to the water, a thin dark line crosses my iphone's screen.

What I see and what the camera stores —
the habit of a woman packing up a kayak
a Japanese maple, its leaves ablaze across the lake
clear water, questions we raise ebbing away.

# Contentions

Each time a writer publishes there is risk to an audience
I have learnt to accept the space a cow inhabits
A school lives on the intuition of its teachers
Jargon in education is the mortar a bricklayer scrapes away
The plastic bags I store in my car boot will outlive me
The view of waves from Tower Hill lifts a person to a height
they are continually striving to reach
You've got to push and shove and grunt and heave in life—
that's all you have to do
I never get money out at the supermarket, they never have the money you want
City poets look at you, smile, but their eyes are elsewhere
Every footballer becomes nostalgic at last
The bum rail in the dairy needs replacing and all
the machinery is being greased before silage and harvesting
All the blinds in town are drawn—it looks like psychosis to me
Some days it is worth fighting for space in your head
Under vast skies, gravel roads disappear at the horizon
I watch my daughters step from change rooms with new clothes—
they advance a year in a moment
Small men in muscle utes like to idle in car parks

# Turning my back on Australians overseas

Trafalgar Square, 4am, waiting
for the night bus to Harlesden.
Sober after another night watching punters
drink and shout to the rhythms of thrash metal.
Like any local I step away from a group
of drunk Australians—as soon as I hear
the accent an inner dread begins,
of being reminded what it is I escaped from—
questions, places, assumptions that I will share
the views of backpackers from Kilmore.
Somehow I avoided cricket, Earls Court
but not the colonial jokes about *Neighbours*.
I left Australia on a one-way ticket
yet the gum trees and paddocks taunt me
as their laughter slips into the chorus from *Flame Trees*
someone's about to chunder. I turn away
as if they were homeless. All I need is historic light
sharpening the walls of monumental buildings
garbos going about their business, the N18 ferrying me
deeper into a one-bedroom flat existence, passengers
dozing off or skinning up, the driver calling out each stop
the Australians' voices in my head, out of whack
with the Danes, Italians and French I wanted to impress.

# Soon there will be townhouses

More than once, I stood on a retaining wall, looked over a paling fence
to the neighbour's inground pool, the al fresco seating area, diving board
deck chairs, Scot's pines casting their shade, the pool that was always full
crystalline, never swam in, an idea to consider from a kitchen window.
Tempted as I was to dive in, I held back to admire from a distance
like those passing chats with the owners and their chooks
each of us unwilling to scratch the surface of what lay between us.

The demolition began at six am, our windows shuddering to a backhoe
spiking concrete pavers, the mottled-brick walls of a 'piece of paradise'
smashed by a steel bucket, roof tiles scattered exposing a hatchwork of battens
and beams.
The pool was drained, broken up, its curved edges dumped
into a waiting truck. A row of Italian pines, severed and mulched.
Any sense of belonging, any connection to land—buried under rubble.
The owner who fed the chooks—a real estate agent—
sold the home to a developer who removed any significant trees
within twelve months before the land was sub-divided.
A process known as the domino effect.

Six months later, weeds and plants are returning like unbidden memories
alyssum, self-seeded canola, dandelion, spinach, lettuce growing wild—
networking underground like the weeds that returned six months after
Hiroshima.
Periodically, workers return to mow the errant plants, to ensure a good gravel
surface.
Soon there will be townhouses, bitumen, concrete, shrubs, a blue chip view—
nothing like the way I looked over a paling fence to an inground pool.

# The truck driver's lament

The town has gone nuts, house prices are un-believe-able.
Locals can't afford to live in town, outsiders come
buy up homes, put them on Air B n B
rent them out for thousands a week.
80% of homes in town are on Air B n B.
There needs to be some regulation, some limits, Jesus
I'm not saying developers shouldn't build houses
or buy homes and rent them out.
I'm not saying that at all.
I mean, it's capitalism, that's the system we've got
happening all over the country—Margaret River
Byron Bay, Lorne, Torquay, Apollo Bay.
Houses are going for over a mill, even though
we're hours from the city
each weekend, all year, local businesses can't get workers—
the workers can't afford to live in town!
All we have are tourists feeding the ducks and taking selfies.
Covid just made it worse, this was on before the virus
pubs and cafes have to shut because their staff are isolating.
The IGA has three posters stuck up on their windows
for Staff Wanted. There are no rentals. Outsiders move to town
work from home or make a killing on Air B n B.
A young single mother was living out of town with her two kids
until the owner sniffed how much he might make.
She was forced to move an hour away
to get another rental, kids are at a new school
away from friends, this is how a community struggles.
I mean, you need locals for Auskick, netball, the Toy Library,
reading at school. What outsiders are going to do that?
My ten year old son, he likes to hang at the local skate park
last week, he and his friends were told to F Off
by a group of 15 year old out-of-towners.

I mean, what 15 year old tells a 10 year old to F Off at a skate park?
Where are the parents? Meanwhile the council
puts on events in town each weekend, but not for locals.
It's capitalism I know, and don't get me started on the government
the two hour wait for a taxi, the two buses a day, oldies not being able to
get to the doctors while this morning a tourist complains that the trees
are slow to turn red or yellow this year and is there some explanation?

# The invigilator's dream

The only sound is of hands shifting along lined paper
some students rest their head on an arm, scribbling.

Preparation can't account for morning light
slanting across brown formica.

He rereads the flyer for emergency evacuation
finds himself standing on a back lane with a road gang—

smell of fresh bitumen, blackened shovels
weatherboard farmhouses dwarfed by over-arching blue.

He leans against the STOP/GO sign
in the days before Hi-Vis he is praying for cars

the silence reasonable like a gap between utterances.
A Mazda pulls up, he eyeballs the driver

turns his STOP sign. Another car arrives
soon he has a queue of three listening to crows.

Time secretes. He is standing on a back road
about to flip a sign. It's as complex as a job can get.

The studious ones are driven by thought
their faces mere inches from the page, black pens

struggling to keep up unlike those who like a laugh
who refuse homework or study. For 100 minutes

they are trapped in a room with red carpeted walls
scratching at what they can remember

and the ones who only write four sentences.
He spins the sign, nods a wave

fully grown into standing around for a living
lost in his head, the red circle, its singular

word haunting him the way a sign turned around
defines his purpose. He squints into a mirage

scuffs his work boots in yellow gravel
crosses time from the whiteboard, collects the papers.

The students are out the door, the room's energy
drains like water swivelling down a basin.

# And

I am standing in ankle-deep water, sunlight
playing across the wavelets, those traces and signatures
of larger waves, running across the sand

circles of light reflecting off the water
mirroring the ribbed patterns beneath
and I am looking at my feet, light
glinting over them like a projection

and I sense the tug of sand
the shelf I've been standing on being called
from between my toes, almost a massage, except
this is land slipping away from me
the slap and drag of the ocean on repeat

and a group of surfers in wetties beyond the breakers
paddling out, duck-diving or perched
on their boards waiting for a set to roll in
timing their rise to stand, carve, twist, cut back and glide
until the wave slumps and then they do it again

paddling out, waiting like the mother calling in
her reluctant son, the girl ferrying water in a bucket
to the castle, the man sunbaking and turning over
each half-hour, the dog walkers and pacers
striding between rock pools at the foot of each headland

and I keep rewriting this poem the way light refracts
across the shallows, returning to the beginning
writing in longhand until I find the form the poem
can live in and something travels from my brain

to my arthritic right hand and I find a foothold
the way a surfer knows when to rise

and while my ankles are dissolving in octagonals of light
just for a moment, I return to forgetting myself

# Midnight Oil at Mt Duneed

hoodies jeans Oils Ts loud tops piercings swagger
queue to the Merch tent screens goatees grey hair
the banter no aggro just tatts no fuss with the over—fifties
families in puffer jackets camp chairs mothers
with adult sons a scattering of masks men who need to stand
to talk clustering with a three day growth sweeping gaze
chairs rugs crackers kids in Oodies sauntering between
food stalls expectations calamari and chips texting a friend
people converging on the arc of portable toilets downward
glance for a moment the Bunnings world held at bay Goanna
as support slip into the nostalgia of Razor's Edge *Torquay Davey*
a generation reflects The Lady Bay when politics was heartfelt
awakening we stand on sloping ground clutching a can
some of us employed in one or two marriages since lyrics
falling from us like syrup heat of a memory flushing the skin
beneath my eyes realizations catching me like a communion
wafer stuck to the roof of my mouth opening riffs of Solid Rock
has strangers dancing grins of recognition repeat of the chords
all around me men are singing badly throwing arms across broad
shoulders some perfecting the mid-50s sway others remembering
how to shuffle each of us knowing how it is to live within three minutes
of a song where a chorus can hold you as the cans pile up
around my feet we keep our distance in the queue for toilets
burgers or Timboon Ice Cream follow the light of our phones
half-believing hope runs the length of a song corrugated iron tank
crush at the front post-lockdown yelps deep and meaningfuls
with strangers on Shane Warne who remembers the first time
they read Sharon Olds stopped for Fool's Gold insert your own
failing Prime Minister a tall bald headed man is waving his arms
frantically at the crowd amped acoustic guitars rhythms from
share-house parties what US Forces does to a circle of arm-flailing friends
I'm drinking sly whiskey with tears my body mainlining the kick

and snare outsiders red dirt First Nations we've been riding these rhythms before simple repeat of da do do do do do do da doo lifts the crowd each person rises arms outstretched yearning with phones bodies falling and rising in unison Garret conducting urging the heaving mass to surge forever upward this unofficial anthem floating spreading with the misting rain

# Here

What they say to you, what they will allow
the way they size you up at the school meet and greet
where nick names are revived to pull you back down.
History is a timeline of a footballer's career
only men talk sport on the radio each Saturday
where the abattoir is the biggest employer in town,
locals know the wind on the crater walk, how to
hang laps of the Dirty Angel, how to huddle
closer to a coach's words.

Cradling a gun gave me the license I needed to kill
to belong if necessary watching kangaroos on the run
ramming themselves into dog fences. Later
I could brood like a local over what I had done.
The cold metallic barrel, dull wood grain stock
stashed in the Cool Room ceiling,
a secret I kept from my father
like a bullet in my pocket, I knew
I was capable of killing what was no longer needed.

Here, a woman checks on her maidens each morning
bottle-feeding, sheltering, pulling a dead lamb from a ewe
pushing a prolapsed uterus back in by hand.
We escape the city to look for more time, a community
where the neighbours are more than a person you wave to.
A bull stands on a dam ridge, an Irish backpacker lifts
the cups to 500 circling Friesians. The country is an idea
shredded by distance, zero rentals. Mist rises off fence posts
the country I am watching, the country I keep driving to.

# Notes

pg 3: The poem, 'Feldspar', is based on The Hazards mountain range overlooking Coles Bay in Tasmania, where the feldspar granite is flecked with iron oxide impurities and which renders the stony sides of the mountain range pink in the afternoon sun.

pg 15: Tin kettlings are mostly a rural tradition where friends gather outside the home of a newly married couple, often just back from their wedding. The friends would bang saucepans and tins outside the house until they were invited inside for cakes and drinks.

pg 43: The title 'Park Life' was inspired by the Blur song of the same name.

pg 49: 'I do this, I do that' takes its title from some descriptions of the American poet, Frank O'Hara's poems set in New York in the 1960s and often characterized by their exploration of daily activities and events. See *Lunch Poems*, Frank O'Hara, City Lights Books.

pg 56: Aradale was a psychiatric hospital in Ararat sometimes referred to as The Aradale Lunatic Asylum. It operated from 1867-1993.

pg 58: The poem, 'Hurt', explores the video for Johnny Cash's cover of the Trent Reznor song. The video was directed by Mark Romanek.

pg 59: Cliff Portwood was an Australian 1970s crooner and a regular on The Mike Walsh Show.

pg 60: Arumpo Road is one of the main unsealed roads that leads to Lake Mungo in NSW.

pg 82: Midnight Oil and Goanna played at Mt Duneed, outside Geelong, March 5, 2022.

pg 84: The title of the poem, 'Here', was inspired by the Philip Larkin poem of the same name.

The Dirty Angel is a statue on a roundabout in Warrnambool that commemorates the services of war veterans and when viewed side-on, the angel appears to be pleasuring herself.

# Acknowledgements

Thanks for the editors of the following publications where some of these poems first appeared:

*Antipodes, Island, Meanjin, Stylus, Foam:e, The Australian., Westerly.*

'Sonnets for a Mother' was Highly commended in the 2020 ACU prize for poetry.

Thanks to Anthony Lynch, Amanda Johnson, Anne Gleeson and Nat O'Reilly for their close reading of poems in the collection.

As always, heartfelt thanks to Lucinda, Ruby and Alison Girvan for their feedback on poems and continued support enabling me to write poetry.

9 780645 651270